Love's

Reflections

By Dudley (CHRIS) Christian

A

Pause For Poetry ©

Publication

Acknowledgement:

Special thanks to my wife, Marilyn Christian for compiling, organizing and finalizing the books of my collections. Her photographing and editing skills were vital to all of my works.

ISBN: 978-0-9916853-0-1

First Edition October 2012
Revised Edition June 2017

Cover Photograph: Author at Mill Lake, Abbotsford, BC © Marilyn Christian

<u>An Opening Word by the Author...</u>

Many people often ask:

"How do you write and do you have to often rewrite your material?"

I have long summed up my answer to the above with the following:

"A Word, the written word, small purveyor of a thought, so like a thought, once thought, cannot be recalled, so too, a word once writ, should need NOT be re-written, for with such licence, we would but change ... the very substance of the thought."

... DNC © 1970

Dudley (Chris) Christian founded and hosted the first and only "PAUSE FOR POETRY" show dedicated solely to the introduction of new and unknown poets and their works. This TV series ran from 1974 to 1985.

Table of Contents

Dear Reader:

Love's Reflections, then, is just what best enlightens one to the stories held in these poems. As you seek to share, or be cognizant of these lines, you will find only one recurring theme, one never-changing, one indistinguishable fact...

LOVE is the answer... ALWAYS... so now what is the question????

A Reflection is a mirror image of a place, person, thought or anything else we put into our minds and then dwell thereon, either through curiosity, thru fate or just our luck in life... Look into a lake, or a mirror... each will but show you back exactly what YOU have placed there, except when you look closely, you will see that it is really a mirrored image appearing for you to view...

So then please look into these ramblings of mine and see in each the true REFLECTION of LOVE calling to you...

...As Love lives on forever
It is Fearless... It is Endless... It is Faultless...
It is Indestructible... It is All-giving...
It is all Encompassing...
Once we have Loved... we never stop loving...
It is the Fool who says... Love has died...
It is the Fool who says... I have lost Love...
It is the Fool who says... I have fallen out of Love...
Love is without Boundaries... Without Shame...
Without Vengeance... Without the capacity for Jealousy

Love sees not its carrier but only...

Those whom it is bestowed...

Love then is the Ultimate form of Expression...

The Ultimate Compliment...

The Ultimate Goal of ALL living things...

Love is Eternal and thereby Eternity...

Love IS God and thereby God is Love...

Love is boundless... Love is healing...

Love is comforting... Love is warmth...

Therefore Love is the only true...

Lasting honest expression of or in life...

To have Loved is to have lived and...

To have lived is to have known Love...

Life... Breath... Existence are All but by-products

Of Love expressed...

Who then can say I am Unloved...

Who then can say I never knew Love...

Who then can say I cannot Love...

Who then can say I Will Not Love...

...Only The Fool...

For be it large or small... Be it good or bad...

Be it right or wrong... Be it whatsoever it may be...

Only the fool rejects the one, ULTIMATE GIFT

Given to All... Only the Fool disallows the Existence...

Of the Elixir of LIFE itself... for...

...ONLY the FOOL, Only the Fool, shuns L O V E...

What Am I Doing Here...

The Loon is a bird whose ever mournful cry
In the still of day
Has been the topic of many a poets verse...
The Loner is a person you or I whose mournful days
In which they still cry is the topic of this poets verse...

****

The foghorns melancholy mourn
The fire and police sirens sound
The crash and crackle of bent automobiles
The screams of children in pain or play
Then silence as the ever-present
Pitter patter of the rain
Beats against the glass patio door
I lay and wonder
What am I doing here... HERE
Here amongst these strangers
Strangers which I so abhorred
Abhorred until I in haste departed
Departed into the quiet solace
Of the far calmer reaches
Of my country home...
Yet City here I lay
Here where I destroy myself
My everything of value
I cast down

Upon a bed of strangeness...
Loner I feel tho near and warm
A body presses hard mine up against
Searching practiced fingers
Seek my desires to rekindle
Painted lips
In false loud passionate words reach for mine
The fulfillment of passion alone
I can and will enjoy
But what of love, respect and dignity
Where have they flown and why...
Where rests they which holds yet my peace and joy
Where now alone feeling lost unwanted
Where now run my loves... my wife... my girl... my boy
Aye City here in deeper thought and self-disgrace I lay
Here in arms which once they are removed
Leave but their shame
Leave but their weight of guilt
Leave me cold and regretful of the day
Loner yes Loner I lay here now
The quiet of the night broken
By screams of law enforcer cars
By emergency machines which haste hereto
To take away from me my shame in bloody blanket clad
But alas the shame it but extends
Enveloping in full

My life my loves my name
No more in secret can my shame remain
My self-disgrace has reached now to cover yet
The only things in life I cared about
And City here with you
In your selfish arms I lay
Here as you bleed my strength
As you exact from my heart
That highest price of all... my pride, my self-respect
How now can I gaze into thy face
How now can I enjoy thy freely given charms
How can I look tomorrow to with you
When in reality I can feel now naught but shame
When rest I in thy arms
What price oh City do you ask
Is but my pride and shame not payment yet enough
Must you like leech stuck still stick
To bleed not just my body, soul and mind
But even yet my young and innocent
Enough oh City close thy door
Retake thy keys
Give not thy number nor address again
Loner here I came and so me you did meet
And stripped so clean
Now City let me go
Let my now worn, tired and aching country heart

Return to its warm enfold and find its rest
Now City let my joys of ages past unseen remain
Let me for but the short while left by fate
Live once with no more shame disgrace nor hate
Release my soul
Release me let my young around me rally
Let me pay on for moments stolen in thy arms
In self shame but in silence
Cast not down what little there be left for those
Those innocents of mine
Who now by my mistakes they too must be engulfed
City... relinquish thy hold on me
Create no pain now for others
Resort not to thy hateful wiles
Loner came I so let me leave alone
Oh City rob not me of life
Thy charms have made my bed
Thy practiced arts has filled my head
With dark and passionate desires
Desires full for but a moment
Then joy departs and shame alone remains
Let me a Loner City go my way
Back to my country alcove
Let me withdraw from thy embrace
Let me this interlude and this forbidden
Rendezvous with you now end

Oh City touch me lightly
Light not again my hidden wants
My animal desires
Touch me not as a prospect for a future catch
Touch me City but only as a friend
Touch me city... touch me in a way
That will allow my love my young
To witness and approve
Touch me in ways Oh City that tells me
Of compassion
A way that leaves me feeling clean
Oh City let my rendezvous with thy dark reaches end
Thy vices and enticements hide me from
Behold my youth... my shame... my love... my life
Loner... aye tho so I be oh City
See me, see me but only as a friend
See me now fair City... but only as a friend
The foghorns melancholy mourn
The fire and police sirens sound
The crash and crackle of bent automobiles
The screams of children in pain or play
Then silence
As the ever-present pitter patter of the rain
Beats against the glass patio door
I lay and wonder, What am I doing here?
What am I doing here...?

Beloved Infidel You Call Me...

An infidel you call me
Beloved tho untrue
Without a heartfelt longing
For love lasting ever true
No thoughts give I for feelings
No love or warmth or such
But rather I keep looking
E'er reaching out to touch
Ah stop but for a moment
And question what you say
If feelings naught I do feel
Why continue on this way
My heart an open book it is
My arms a fortress strong
My love a fire burning is
Waiting some love to come along
For years and hearts I have known
In haste and fitful hurry
Who had but little time to give
Who for my life felt but sorry
Yet sorry tho I may have seemed
Myself ne'er so has been
For after every shattered dream
I've stood tall and tried again

Until alas now here I stand

With heart open unveiled

Once more to fall or onward stand

Waiting fate to be revealed

Beloved infidel I am

Tho I chose not to be

Beloved yes that was my plan

Infidel has been my destiny

Beloved infidel I'll be... until the times bring true

A true and warm and lasting love

Maybe... It will be you...

"I So Hate to Love and Leave You"

I SO HATE TO LOVE AND LEAVE YOU
BUT I REALLY GOTTA GO

With these words

Her voice like heaven

Cut so short the music sweet

Broke the fragile bond between us

As she made her shy retreat

As the electronic marvel

Of our age lay silently

In my hands where seconds earlier

It had brought her near to me

Fragile bits of wire metal

All enclosed protectively

From the reaches of life's elements

A bridge so slender

'Twix you and me...

I SO HATE TO LOVE AND LEAVE YOU
BUT I REALLY GOTTA GO

Mere words used in conversation

I tell myself it isn't so

Reach into their realms

And find there

Meanings, feelings hidden each

Look there message for unspoken

As one heart tries yours to reach

Press the phone

Hard to your lips now

Close your eyes

Visualize

Other lips across the chasm

Pressing warmly

'Neath closed eyes...

I SO HATE TO LOVE AND LEAVE YOU
BUT I REALLY GOTTA GO

In my ears as a reminder

Echo these words

O'er and o'er

In platonic rendezvous

Safe and secure our love endures

Tho we meet we never touch

Loving full each other

Pure

Times -- they call us

Life's situations

Each apart at times we be

Yet in the reaches

Of fond feelings

Ever near in memories

Rush you then unto your callings

'Til we another time shall meet

Be it while at home

Or while yet working

Or on life's ever busy street

Keep your voice sweet and happy

Call me back to talk awhile

Let me hear your angels whisper

Thrill me with your warming smile

I SO HATE TO LOVE AND LEAVE YOU
BUT I REALLY GOTTA GO

I SO HATE TO LOVE AND LEAVE YOU
I KNOW I TOO HAD BETTER GO...

And So Having Showered

And so having showered
And myself perfumed in soaps and oils
Feel rested from my aches and pains
Then tho with face four days in splendid growth
I reach and take the blade
The soap and brush
Lather fast the growth I've come to pride
Watch as the whiskers
Stand like stalwarts in the soap
Their one last glorious stand
Before the blade across them moves

And moving onwards fast
The blade in haste
Removes my stubble growth of beard
The beard which but for days four
Stood adorning
The lower now clean circumference of my face
But ah alas peace has returned
Serenity and coos soft filled with love
As my body and my ears can rest in peace
From these females incessant chatterings
And complaints
As dotingly they press their hairless faces
Softly mine up against...

You're Married...

You're married...
Aye, so it seems, and so am I but yet
How strange it matters not
Your eyes become a heavenly book
Your hearts voice speaks in every look
You give

Ah... but sigh not my pretty one
The nights Moon follows close the setting Sun
To bid deeply to those that sigh with lonely tears
Hidden 'neath a sparkling eye...
A promise

Aye a promise of the rest of night
Of coming dawn of new days bright
Of things we once had dreamed like now
Of full and free and lasting love
Take not this tiny bit of thought
For slur or jest from one who oughtn't
But seek within your hidden fears
Re-visit all your hurts and pains
Then think of one who as thou art
Must live so near yet be apart
Away, away, away from life
Away from love next door to strife
Next door to all that casts one down
To e'er be trampled 'neath the ground
Of joyous pain or sorrow
And now it seems we two must part
And will not meet tomorrow.

The Void God Couldn't Fill...

I recall the face of loneliness
Which upon a child I saw
Who lived in a broken home
Separated from its pa (ma)
The smile of surface only
Adorned its features sweet
Yet one could so clearly see
The beating broken heart beneath
In words so hollow and so cold
Like the lost bleating of a lamb
Trying to excuse its emptiness
Accepting life as best it can
Still one the strangeness beheld
With every word or step taken
As for the filling of its void
Consistently the child kept reaching
The father (mother) which it lived on with
Tries hard both roles to play
Still try as he (she) might 'twas useless
That void fully to take away
With vacation trips and fancy clothes
Games all and schools so fair

He (she) tries to reach and filter in

With loving words and cares

Material things which money could

The best of all 'twas bought

Yet tho in pleasing gratitude taken

Unfilled remain reaction sought

'Til then in final quest for life

That roamer cast aside

Of this world it's hoped for things

Sought one him (her) to stand besides

And empty life seemed fulfilled

But to this man (woman) who lived alone

Still empty that child remained

That heart void of a home

Then in desperation reaching out

The last stand for hope he (she) tried

To God his (her) life he (she) gave

Trying to happy make this child

The ways of life all now changed

As better than good he (she) grew

Waiting patiently but to see

Joy in the child he (she) knew

Had I But Now the Time...

Had I but now the time
To get to know you better
E'er you walk on before me
A picture out of life
Which so fully lie enveloped
By clean cascading hair
O'er shoulders small petit
Transparent bell umbrella
Your loveliness protecting
From cold winter's rain
Now falling as in sleet
Full clad are you in feminine attire
So seldom seen today
Looking like a dream unending
From pleasant night
To rainy day
Alas too soon you'll pass
E'er but a whispered word
Exchanged
Had I but now the time
Had I but now the time
Had I but only now the time
To get to know you better
Before you leave again forever...

Yet Lo and Behold...

Yet lo and behold

The sounds of nature all entwine

To form sweet music

As they fall upon the ear

'Tis but the magic mating call

Which falls

With uniformity

Full from each matched pair

And be it squeal of pig

Or call of cat in heat

Loud chirping of a bird without a nest

Yet be it buzz

O'er flower of a bee

Or horses hooves a'galloping in the west

Or cooing softly

Of a turtle dove

Or loud or soft cries

Of women in the night

The sounds of nature all the same

In uniformity

All intertwine

In peace

Contentment

Harmony and love...

Women Are a Peculiar Lot...

Women are a peculiar lot
This I've come to find
Their logic is beyond compare
With that of we mankind
In silent playful waiting
They lay 'til man comes 'round
Then act so uninterested
'Til man disgusted is outbound
Now watch their "stop there" glances
Their eyes with promises filled
The little lost and lonely look
Which many a heart has chilled
And man stops... does their bidding
Awaits on their every whim
To please and happy keep them
A sole purpose in life for him

Women are a peculiar lot
Take when a single man they meet
Though he has two or other three
Sees them maybe once a week
Tho full knowing of the others
Whom with the nights will spend
No mention of her in anger
Will she make to him offend

Women are a peculiar lot
If a mistress is paused upon
Full knowing that her lover has
And sleeps with a wife at home
No grievance for the spent moments
Which upon his wife he'll place
No tears nor pain nor anger
Just love and smiles upon her face

Women are a peculiar lot
When a divorced man roams about
He seems to bring the sensuousness
Hidden deep in each woman out
Unspoken promises of fulfillment
Such as he'd never known
A future forgetful of the past
If he takes her for his own

Yes, women are a peculiar lot
As marriage quickly shows
For no sooner has vows been taken
Than a ring goes thru man's nose
No more to look too closely
At other females that abound
Nor even think to take a night
Alone out on the town

Fully tied and domesticated he
Must be content now with one
Her every whim and wish to fill
Or his world she will tear down
And quite as suddenly as before
Her promises she showed free
Become bargaining tools e'en now
As no competition now has she

Her pants of passion and desire
Becomes words of hate and slur
As he is assured his wants and desires
Is now but mere duty unto her

Women are a peculiar lot
Once they have had their way
Their charms like claws are withdrawn
While their claws see light of day
They bring to mind the nesting bird
Which sings so sweet all day
In promises of coming spring
Which takes the cold away
And like the singing bird they chirp
'Til their nest with eggs are filled
Then like the birds in silent rest
Their loud passionate noises stills

Women are a peculiar lot
Tho any age they be
If long you for her charms to last
Then leave her ever free
For once you place upon her hand
The rings security shows
Her charms will leave in silent flight
While the rings go thru your nose...

This Year There'll Be No Forever

This year there'll be no forever
Tomorrow will pass like today
We'll go on our way
Full, happy and gay
The way we both know we should be
This year there'll be no forever
No bad memories as you from me part
But nestled instead
In my arms rest your head
As your love lies here in my heart
This year there'll be no forever
Nor more tears or sorrows to know
Each day now we'll live
All the love that life gives
And forever love's all we will know.

<u>Since You Feel Yourself Not Good Enough...</u>

Since you feel yourself not good enough

For me to even speak to

Then my heart for you bleeds

For the loss you will have known... For

For I have talked with Princes

And I have walked with Governors

And at the Princess' table

A place for me they set

Yet I have been a prisoner

Been bruised, enslaved and beaten

Still ne'er thru it all

Have I lost self-respect

I've lain with every nation

Each type and class of women

Brought joy and never pain

Where down I rest my head

The young I have befriended

The old share me their wisdom

The poor still grace my table

While the rich glad pay my wage

Mankind has taught me often
Has often learnt too from me
Has looked at me as equal
All past 'til along you came
Now with your snobbish glances
You silently walk by me
As if you are not good enough
To speak or breathe our air
Some others may think different
But I've traversed too widely
This world and come to know
The guilt, shame and fear you bear
I can't condone the past that's been
I can forgive the future
Look at you now as human
If you meet me halfway
So shed your inferiority
Let go your guilty complex
Join in our conversations
So we nevermore shall say...

Since you feel yourself
Not good enough
For me to even speak to
Then my heart for you bleeds
For the loss you will have known...

Oh Daffodil Your Beauty Is Enshrined...

Oh daffodil your beauty is enshrined
And often praised you be in poets rhyme
Your golden loveliness a wonder e'er
Which seems to grow in splendour
Yet with time
Thy long and frail green upright stem
Like leg upon a maiden fair
In flight
Sway... with a cape loose long
Around your head
Where golden curls fall
Moonbeam-like left and right
In folds of wonder deep
Your honeycup
Enfolds around
Thy budding pollen pods
While swanlike
Your proudly bend but slight
Thy neck and head
In reverence unto God

Oh daffodil your beauty is enshrined
As it so deserving e'er should be
In verse and song and tribute fine
In ode in oil in loving memory
How could I then pass by thy way

With ne'er a hand outstretched
To touch
With ne'er a pause for moment still
Once more my life by you
To be enriched
Then pardon please
My guilty move
As quick I snap thy stem
And short thy life
In seeming uselessness
First close to my heart
Your beauty once to hold
Then lovingly... You
Into my lovers hands
I press...

E-L-I-Z-A-B-E-T-H... the Fairy's Chant...

One glance in your eyes
Large **lovely** and bright
One look at your nameplate I knew,
The whisperings of fairies
To gods lost in the woods
Spoke clearly and dearly of you,
E L I Z A B E T H
Your name
E L I Z A B E T H
Like their chanting the same

ELIZABETH

The letters all clinging in unison full,
Brought back for a moment
My thoughts of past days
When I'd worship those chant-like words too,
Elizabeth... Elizabeth.
"Elizabeth, Elizabeth
A sweeter woman ne'er drew breath
Than my son's fair wife
Elizabeth"
Some poet of age old
Some master of the arts
Once wrote those words so alone,
To a lovely but cold cold lover
Which from him death had taken
And he cried over her tablet of stone.
Elizabeth, Elizabeth, Elizabeth.
Now here in the flesh alive
Again I have found,
That princess of fairies who'd flown
To die once, before her true lover
In his arms she could take,
To cherish as always his own.
Elizabeth
Still time has renewed you,
Elizabeth
In vibrance and joy
To fill once again

So it seems,
This void left so empty
When last you did fly,
From fulfillment
Of love's happy dreams.
So be you now princess or fairy
Or just lonely or lover or girl,
Or nothing which on I have touched,
Still your eyes and your smile
Brought warm memories recalled,
So much.
Elizabeth, Elizabeth
A whisper soft of wind
Elizabeth, Elizabeth
A bird's song on the air
Elizabeth, Elizabeth
The rustle of leaves on a tree
Elizabeth, Elizabeth
Water cascading down (green) a mountainside
All echo to me so hauntingly.
Elizabeth, Elizabeth
A finer woman ne'er drew breath
Elizabeth, Elizabeth
Their song ** your name
Becomes my breath,
Elizabeth, Elizabeth
Forever your name's on my breath...

"Ode to Pretend"

We met one day in a hurry
And like a storm you entered my mind
I held to you but didn't believe
That my life was real for a time
It amazes me as I think now
Of the fast way you on me fell
Like a dream it seemed
While you were with me
And more like a dream
Since you've left
I guess I knew at the onset
That not for awhile would you stay
But it seemed to me
That tho I dreamed it might be
To live a bit on in pretense
I pretend that one night I held you
So close to me soft and warm
I pretend that one time I heard you
Say you'd see me again if I called
I pretend that one day I phoned you
And heard your sweet voice sleepy say
I'll be here again later waiting
Please call me again later today
I pretend that I sat by the pay phone

And called to you each half hour long

'Til the constant ringing and ringing

'Gainst empty walls tore me down

I pretend that then I in a trancelike

Did to your place quickly go

To watch and wait in pretensions

That sooner or later you'd show

I pretend that I left you a message

When all of my waiting proved vain

I pretend that I don't really hurt now

And that my lone hours hold me no pain

I pretend that prehaps on the 'morrow

I'll see you again one more time

For if ever I stop these pretensions

I'd pretend that I've lost my mind.

Forever with my entire being
Until your Mother Nature
Who gave you beauty
And your Father Time
Who gave you wisdom
Relinquish to us the destiny
We must one day share

Moon Who Takes Your Hand

Moon who takes your hand
And leads you as you go
Across the wide expanse of sky
To the strange places that you know
Who keeps you company I ask
As each night in the lonely sky
You shine down bright in heavenly light
As each land you pass by
You never stop or e'en complain
When mortals block you out
With their ideas which cause pain
And pollution the world about
But still your endless splendour
At every chance it can
Shines down so bright and lovingly
On us ungrateful man
I've often wondered deeply
If you should from us part
What would become of all our land
Would our world then fall apart
Would our seas and rivers leave us
Or in a watery grave us send
Would the mountains fall into the sea
And bring us to our end
Would heavens stars fall on us

In showers hailstone like
To forever kill and crush us
Like we crushed your light at night
Oh Moon upon the waters blue
Send on your silvery beams
You're much yet to
Those who look for you
In life and love and dreams

A Portrait of Long Yesteryear

A portrait of long yesteryear
Your face draws back to me
A time a space in life and time
When yet my heart grew free
Eyes so like yours did thrill me
As they gazed deep into my own
Therein I saw your thoughts deep
Intermixed alive alone
Then faint and shy it spread thin
A smile played in your face
Til cherry lips slow parted
And I your tongue they did taste
Then heaven blessed the moment
As its choir to me soft played
And your voice broke thru my consciousness
Here with me to in memory stay

Oh to Be Young Again

Oh to be young again and free --free
Free to see the world again
In shades of black & white
Free and young to believe
To believe again
In a realistic mono affair
Young and innocent enough
To escape into fantasies
Young and free to wait on
For fulfillment of dreams
Ah to be young again
And free -- free
Free in thought and mind
Free to love and be in love
With love itself
Young enough to imagine
Each as never-ending
Naive enough to believe
It will prevail
To dream that its thrill
Will never fade
And tomorrow shall ne'er
For a moment temptation show
Ah yes to be young again

Young and free -- free
Free in spirit to believe
Free in will to carry on
Free to look unseeing
Into life's experiences
And criticize the old
Free to assure the elders
That your future's yours
To Shape, to Mold, to Hold
Young and free to speak out
On any topic yet in wisdom full
Young and free to see deceit
As but a weakness of the old
To believe life a path of roses lie
But to perfume your footsteps
As you skip happy by
Oh to be young again
And free -- free
Free to see the World again
In shades of black & white
Free and young to believe
To believe again
In a realistic mono affair.

"Just a Wisp of Wind"

Just a wisp of wind
On a cool spring-wintry day
Just a cloud or two on high
As gulls in the heavens play
Just a ripple soft rolls on
O'er the calm blue sea
Just a glimmer of sunlight
That soon we all shall see
Just a few trees bending heads
As in playful repose they sit
Just a flag so lazily tossed
Like a lady's hair who sits
Watching for the new day
When the time shall last
Looking for a lasting way
To relive fond memories past
Just a thought in passage
Written firm upon the brow
Just a moment of loves message
Being sent to one we love
Oh to be full able free
To live in full content
Doing what my heart asks of me
Living life to its extent
But alas 'tis morning 'gain
And the day's begun
Just a wisp of wintry wind
As we watch the rising sun.

Tho You Knew I Wasn't Free

Tho you knew I wasn't free

Yet you fell in love with me

And blinded all my pains with your sweet love

You made me feel secure

I could forget her now for sure

But the aches come back now what can we do

We didn't mean to have a child

At least not for a while

For that means a bond which we must somehow keep

But life laughed at us with scorn

Ever since our child was born

For in our loveless lives we'll now forever weep

Our child is not to blame

And of you I'm not ashamed

Tho you feel so helpless and inside so dead

And tho I still love you so

You'd be glad to let me go

But to leave my child would drive me from my head

So our past has caught us fast

In a union that must last

Tho our lives will a misery be

For tho you knew I wasn't free

Yet you fell in love with me

But I'll take the blame for our misery

Oh Give Me the Land That I Love

Oh give me the land that I love
The beautiful warm Tropic seas
Where forever I can lie contentedly
Caressed by warm Caribbean breeze
Give me the sands so clean and white
Where the labouring seamen stay
Happily working day and night
Thru moonshine or heat of day
Give me the girls so sweetly dressed
In their colourful native style
With soft dark hands I've loved to press
Since I was but a tiny child
Oh give me the birds in the treetops
Singing their songs of love
Bringing joy to all mankind
Straight from our Lord above
That's why my mind does wander
As I sail upon these seas
My home in the West Indies
Oh home in the Tropic Islands
Where ne'er alone did I stray
I long to relive those happy years
Never more to move far away
Oh my little Tropic Isle
Cooled by the North-East breeze
'Twas home to me in my childhood days
Kneeling there by my father's knees
Yes I love my little Isle
And that's why I beg you please
Keep me no longer far away
From my home in the West Indies

"Comfort Stop"

A white snow-covered grassy knoll
Where winds on pink flowers play
As silent smoke flows overhead
Waterfalls softly wind their way

Two trees full bare on trunks they be
With roots full planted firm
Their limbs each other intertwine
As the winds slow rock the boughs
In nest of birds above the limbs
A beaute of beak stands out
As sweet chirping music sounds forth
Playing long each bluebird about
Long moss dark moss like maidens hair
From topmost perch hangs down
Enveloping the nest and birds
Three sides it doth surround
Then as the water ceases flow
The white snow slowly spreads
'Til all the grassy knoll is covered
Leaving just the pink flower heads
The foliage all around spring up
To hide from view the trees
And all that's left for vision now
Is hanging moss and covering leaves
The birds they flutter and are still
The music sweetly fades.
The forest of life has swallowed again.
The beautiful young bare maid.

Veronica... the Fairy Child...

A whisper of the weather
A warm breeze softly blowing
A thought of bygone ages
These all I keep recalling
A far off land like heaven
With bright and sunny skies
A sea warm yet at midnight
Now for my heart oft cries
Then like the past re-opened
You vision-like appear
I hear your name Veronica
Come drifting thru the air
I close my eyes -- I see you
Your full dark hair and eyes
I think back and I feel you
Warm near here by my side
I reach out and I touch you
The skin I lived to touch
Your name returns to me again
Which I whispered once so much
And as now I stand lonely
The wind it seems to say
Veronica... Veronica...
Then goes it on its way
Above my head the singing bird

Chirps sweet and loud its call
Veronica... Veronica...
Resounds throughout the hall
Rush then I to the waterfall
As the fountain softly plays
A tattoo called Veronica
It seems to constant say
Maybe crazy I've become
Obsessed by you I seem
Your haunting name it follows me
By day in sound by night in dreams
You of whom the ancients said
Was by the fairest fairy borne
Veronica named for their Queen
Truly it seems one you've become
Veronica... Veronica...
Still loud to me you call
Veronica... Veronica...
You the fairest still of all.

You can't run on and on forever
Tho as a mountain climber you won't stop
Remember as you climb on
Even the tallest mountain has a top

"Noel... Christmas Child..."

Oh Christmas child I had you named
So full of hopes for life
You filled my life for but awhile
Yet made it all since right
You took the wild part of my being
Made it stable and secure.
For which it seems I gave you naught
But a name and life unsure
Oh Christmas child I've held you once
To my heart so warm and near
Yet thru the years since gone on
You'll always remain here
A long and distant land apart
We stay for years on end
Yet you're always close here in my heart
So why should I pretend
The seasons all again have passed
From Spring thru Summer 'n' Fall
'Til once again the years last end
Brings the silent first snows fall
It's times like these I miss you most
You the joy which first I knew
Your warm self held so close to me
That first time I held you

Alas fate moved and me removed

To live from you apart

Yet tho the miles us separate

You're close here in my heart

As this time of year it calls

Home echoes all return

It's time when Christmas' in the air

I miss you most my son

I'll sit again and watch the snows

So soft and cold fall down

To cover all the evergreens

The last of Autumn's reds and browns

I'll watch the streams and rivulets

So slowly to ice turn

And wish to share them once with you

As father with a son

I'll stare out into space

And see what could have been

Yet all that I can hope for now

Is to one day call you friend

So many years in silence I

Have sat as 'lone you grew

Dying inside but unable here

To reach out a hand to you

Yet as the Christmas time it nears

Still I wait with hopes to see

That tiny card which always comes
Which says you still love me
Yes son the snow is falling now
The Winter's cold draws nigh
I pause again with you in thoughts
As I gaze up to the sky
If there be one who lives up there
As his day we celebrate
He'll take this fathers love to you
Tho the miles us separate
And far across the lands and seas
You'll feel a warming glow
Which says I'm there at Christmastime
To spend each one son with you
So picture as you gaze alone
Me gazing alone too
I in your thoughts as you in mine
Each wishing we were home
Oh Christmas Child I called your name
For that 'twas my favourite season
Now alas alone it is son so cold
As I search on for the reason...
Oh Christmas child I had you named
So full of hopes for life
You filled my life for but awhile
Yet made it all since right

"How Long -- Not Long"

"How long -- not long"
A champion said
As he tried in peace to lead
His trodden down and beaten flock
Away from vengeful acts and deeds
"How long -- not long"
The echo grew
As the cries shattered the skies
As in non-violent protest march
For basic rights the champion tries
"How long -- not long"
A non-battle cry
For soon soon "We Shall Overcome"
Soon soon the way will open be
To enjoy freedom here at home
"How long -- not long"
His promise rang
"For mine eyes the land have seen
My cup is full 'til it overflows
I believe" for "I have a dream"
"How long -- not long"
Let us then rejoice
For in peace we tall shall stand
Equal free in love and dignity
Here with all our fellowman

"How long -- not long"

'Twas a joyful cry

But too filled of truth and fact

Too hopeful for a removal fast

Of deep hatred for the blacks

"How long -- not long"

Then a shot rang out

And to the ground a leader fell

A lone gunman ran -- part of a plan

Of which he would never tell

"How long -- not long"

His echo remains

As the swelling crowd killed and burned

As the last vestige of peacefulness.

The white man again had spurned

"How long -- not long"

Now a sound renewed

Now a meaning changed in full

Now a hand on a Molotov cocktail

Now just waiting a trigger to pull

"How long -- not long"

What a hope filled call

Those words had brought to me

We who were stolen victims all

At last from our abductors would be free

"How long -- not long"

They called you king

And of true royalty you hail
You gave your living and your life
Let us not his dream let fail
"How long -- not long"
Our champion said
Stand tall and renew that shout
We have a dream to dream on with
To push hate, fear and prejudice out
"How long -- not long"
Martin Luther King
Will you walk on slow ahead
We too will make that mountaintop
On that Promised Land we'll tread
"How long -- not long"
We know now for sure
For our guide ahead has gone
His trials all by faith overcome
We shall overcome and follow on
"How long -- not long"
For our future looms
As a bright and shining day
"How long -- not long"
If we keep those words
In our hearts and minds each day
"How long -- not long"
"How long -- not long -- not long"

<u>Love... Life... Women... &... Cars...</u>

A man so often will go to a car lot see a car and take it
for better or worse. It's good while it's going,
you'll never know when it's going to go bad on you,
it's lovely to look at decorated or in a new dress of paint
and it's always wanting something new. It's always ready
when you're not, late when you're in a hurry,
gets really moody at times and just won't move.

Other times it purrs like an angel keeps you ahead of the
others and makes you more proud of it. You see the model
ask the year and pridefully take it home. For the first few
months it's constantly being pampered and given everything
it needs and desires. Then you get to know each other so
well that the slightest noise made by it is detected. It can
keep food out of your mouth and clothes off your back as
long as it has a want with all else being second place.

If it keeps quietly going for too long your belief that
it will never go bad soon gets your eyes looking at other
models on the market. You're forever comparing its
benefits, looks, durability and age with that beautiful
young last or this year's model. You can treat it bad or
good but heaven help anyone else who scratches, or dents

---

or tries to drive it. After faithful service nevertheless unless you've grown pretty old together you will trade it in and naturally take up one of those new models only to find you have the same things to tolerate though admittedly the new model does look better even tho it's much less durable and surely less dependable.

If it up and dies you will put it in a convenient dump where it will soon be forgotten as you make room for your new model, if it lives too long you'll either put it in a rest home (your back yard likely) where it in jealously sulking silence can do nothing but lay around and watch you and your newly chosen model or else you'll find some less fortunate than yourself who hoping for a good thing willingly takes the aged thing off your hands much to your financial relief and mental pleasure.

Down deep friend be careful tho for after all in a jealous rage this sweet little thing can cause you so much... tremendous financial trouble, physical injury or even death with just about nothing you can legally do against it. So be careful if you abuse or misuse it or it in its anger will make you pay dearly...

Does that sound like a wife as well...? Sorry...

United States of America...

I have come from small beginnings

I have lost hate's holding powers

I have grown from pain and slavery

To achieve man's greatest hour

I am known to all the nations

As home of the brave and free

I have spread my glorious banner

From sea to shining sea

I have helped the poor and hungry

I have fought the hard and strong

I have bent beneath their ridicule

Admitted when I was wrong

I've given hope to the hopeless

Tried my best to cast a light

To set an example whereby

All men could as one unite

Thru 200 years I've managed

To give dreams of utopia

Keeping united all my children

I am

United States of America...

There's a Very Thin Line Drawn

There's a very thin line drawn
'Tween convicted and accused
Yet this line allows
Outspoken one to say
The words or charges which
Against me are upbrought
Are true in fact
Or in fact false are they
Then when all words are spoken
And the evidence is nigh
The Judge must weigh the solitary question WHY...?

There's but a very thin line drawn
'Tween right and what is wrong
And often times
The situation is to blame
So 'fore one is wronged
Or declared to be right
One should review
The facts all once again
And once our stand is taken
We it then must stand by
Ne'er compromise our principles
Stand our ground and ask firmly WHY...?

There's a very thin line drawn
'Tween a Parrot and a child
When in its younger months
It's taught to obey
To learn to walk
To eat to frolic
And at last a few words
To mimic say
Yet tho in time soon
That child will cease its cry
When wanting something which
For it may ask
One common factor stands it out
When given any reason
Says straight to you of your task WHY...?

There's a very thin line drawn
'Tween a free man and a slave
It's the line that makes a man
Of you and I
It's the making of a Communist
Or retention of our lives
It's the age old question... WHY?

Why... takes away the blindness
Which a closed society seeks
Why... gives to all its subjects
The right and will to speak

Why... tears down traditions
Which did dominate for years
In keeping man enslaved... From youth
Throughout his years unto his grave
Why... clears the mind of guilt
Which some on it has instilled
Why... makes a life fulfilled
Which long has had no will
Why... keeps a nation growing
As communists stagnate and die
By demanding of their peoples
Just obey and don't ask WHY...?

Why... leaves the young to grow free
To be that which they choose
To love and marry who they will
Others choices to refuse
Why... gives to all their freedom
To seek pinnacles on high
With just one quest on their minds
That quest the freedom... WHY?
There is a thin line drawn
'Tween being and have been
You are the one who draws it
You your own enemy or friend
You are the only one who can
Change your life as it goes by
Your fate and destiny are yours
With freedom to ask... WHY...?

Before Old Bligh Went A-Sailing

Before old Bligh went a-sailing
Cooke as a captain stood
Throughout the Wild West Indies
Set he out to furnish food
From Antilles to Cuba
From Settlement to town
Each Slave-laden place he stopped at
To plant the breadfruit down
A man there was amongst them
Who helped to plant the trees
But in his leisure moments
He busy planted seeds
His seed it full did flourish
There in that fertile land
And by his name they called it.

So Christian came to La Caiman
The sod he placed his seen in
'Twas of Slave an African kind
A mulatto looking female youth
Was what he'd sought to find
No thought gave he thereafter
As on his journey far he'd speed
His seed would go to foster yet
More seed and young unfreed
Back went he then to England
Where from on future trip

He'd learn to thirst for freedom
Yearn to give oppression ship
He'd wait silently while dying
Inside, at what he'd seen
Then in true Christian fashion
He'd lead those that would follow
To a land new where freedom lay
And there they'd build a homeland
Where e're free would remain they
His offspring gave his name to
Slave daughters and Slave sons
And lived to see it bestowed
On grandchildren one by one
Of these there was a woman
Who was called Marry by name
And as she never married
Her Son wore Christian as last name

The man whom her child did father
Was of age old Carib stocks
The fierce and proud and hardy
Who in slavery deep was locked
The offspring of a slave maid
When at her breast he fed
The words of emancipation
In England were being said
Within walls of the castle
He spent his younger days

Where his parents all had toiled
Where they all were kept as Slaves
A friend and comrade Aaron
Whom with he used to play
Would remain fore'er in history
As the isles last runaway
As man with freedom newfound
He'd find his friend once more
Dead weeks with spear and machetes
Sitting by his lean-to's door
And there beneath the good earth
He'd lay the body down
That slave true free forever
Where no one could hunt him down
Then laying out a section
This man did a garden plan
A silent lasting tribute
To Slave Aaron his fellowman.

Away to seek a fortune
In the ways of ships at sea
He left a woman pregnant
With a child who fathered me
The child grew with the old name
Of Herbert Jackson as his dad
Remaining so 'till he was grown
Then changed Jackson for what his mother had

Thus was it that old Fletcher's name
Would last to stand again
Another Christian for England to fight
To help free his fellowmen

The year now 1940
The man grown to twenty five
Went off to fight for England
And at Trinidad did arrive
'Twas there he met a maiden
Of pure black velvet sheen
With hair and eyes black as night
A native of Port-au-Spain
Life's course did run and shortly
This woman for spouse he took
He now a fresh young soldier
She who taught in school the book
He like her of races many
Both from a slave background
He from the Indian slave group
She direct from Africa cast down
She who did know her granpapa
Who from Africa was taken
Inside a woman who was wife
Of French Admiral Gauntaume it's been spoke
For Gauntaume had seen Napoleon
Fight bitter battles past
He knew they could no more fight
He knew their war was lost

So taking his black African
Whose beauty was surpassed
By none of the ladies he had seen
Thru all the places he had passed
And seeking out a safe refuge
Wherein they, he might secure
He chose the island Trinidad
Where his offsprings all she bore

His offsprings set their seed about
Mixed with the natives there
One chose a black Spanish ex-slave
Who to him a girl did bare
This girl grew (up) to womanhood
A teacher good and bright
And married a young soldier who
Came here to help England fight
Two sons she bore this soldier
Before the war was done
Five offsprings more thereafter
Me -- I was the second son.

We left while I an infant lay
Upon her loving breast
Back to my father's homeland
Where she later bore the rest
Grand Cayman now they called it
Tho it had once been known

As La Tortuga and Caimens
Before it was by England owned
Here grew I and the others
In happy ignorance
Content to hold whites as better
Content to pursue no other plans
So well inbred they held us
That no thought gave we of rights
We must be humble and respectful
For after all they were the whites
Such childhood as I recall
'Sides that spent in work or prayers
Was filled with seeking out one white
As friend to ease our fears.

For if just one would let us
Be seen with them around
We'd be at least accepted
Until he put us down
In ways of bribe and cunning
In lies and in deceit
We helped the whites around us
Anything just their friend to be
Yet I recall that somehow
There would be still the fights
As whites from town would send out
Their black friends we blacks to fight
Then they in jolly laughter

Would join and watch us fall
As we beat up on each other
No whites, just we, blacks all
And I recall when eleven
I'd be in just two weeks
I received my first paycheck then
Twelve dollars for four weeks

Since then I've worked and striven
Myself to better make
I've paid for all my knowledge
I've paid for each mistake
I worked until I would earn
In times less than a week
Four times my father's monthly
His Government job was so bleak
For all those years he had been
A worker for the crown
Now at his highest pay scale
Two hundred dollars he held down
Seven children and a wife home
A car and all his needs
From this he must take sustenance
And help his aged parents feed

Nine years I watched him working
Each day without relief
No breaks, no times, no holiday
In pain in want in grief

Then one day I was reading
A tourist board pamphlet
When I chanced to rest upon
This printed unto it
"From overseas a couples needs"
If claims could but be paid
On three hundred fifty dollars then
Including food, shelter, fun and maid
I asked myself the question then
If this they could recommend
What of my poor old father
Why paid he so little them
Then seeking out my answers
I came to fully realize
His worth and value lay to them
In colour to their eyes

I slowly then did understand
What of he had oft spoke
I grasped the meaning of difference
Such of which the white man joke
I heard again my grandfather
Recall to me his youth
And all the tales his father told
Of slavery and its truth
My skin did crawl
My hair did stand
My blood began to boil

I now at last could understand
The whys of all their toil
I vowed then evermore that I
Would set the truth out free
Until my people realized
They should stand only proud and free
The stories each like pictures flashed
In each the same was plain
The black had been the slave downcast
The white had caused the pain
How then I said in anger full
Can justice this way stand
The victim is to prison sent
While the culprit's a free man
How can my people be so blind
To still look to white for help
Our only help is in ourselves
Black Man rise and save yourself
For you thru centuries wronged have been
By those who o'er you rule still
These who speak of laws and justice
While our kind for years they kill
You Black Man child of Africa
Whose parents gave their best
Look to your past in deepest pride
Look to your dead with full respect
Recall their cries in anguish when
They as slaves from Africa came

Chained by some white inside a ship
Black man this holds no shame
Be man and woman boy and girl
Like they once of us said
If but one drop of African blood
Course thru your veins and head
Then Black forever proud and free
Stand fast for all that's been
Fight 'til the White Man leave us be
Fight 'til we're all free men.

Oh Fletcher I could curse you
For your past part in my life
But you redeemed yourself to me
In your mutiny for man's rights
You stood out tall and proudly
As all called Christian always will
You left your country and your home
'Cause you stood on your belief
And England in her glory
Built then on Black man's blood
Could not find or harm you ever
You'd beaten them and good
So 'stead in praise I hold you
Esteemed for your last stand
That's why your name lives on now
In the heart of this Black man

I Need Not Friend to Seek Your Love...

I need not friend to seek your love

Nor beg your hand to hold

I crave not for your wealth or warmth

While I live alone so cold

I've too long lived and learned to be

The man I am... unknown

To ever stoop on bended knee

To reach what I didn't own

In times mayhap our paths may pass

And me you'll chance to know

Until that time I ask but this

Judge not what you do not know...

Take not the words of those about

As truth filled gospel fact

It may just be that they regret

Never being part of the act

For few and scarce are those that I

Would choose for friends from these

Tho on speaking terms I do remain

I seek no one here to please

I live and love I meet and part
Sometimes regret when I must go
But of those who has called me friend
Judge not what you don't know

Take not my life as they have seen
Within their hate filled minds
And equate there one moment friend
With the truth of this life of mine
But rather if your call is loud
To find the answers true
Stay not behind your masks so proud
Come show all the real you
Then once you have your evidence
You as friend can stay or go
And you like few that you will meet
Can judge what you do true know...

> Marriage is like a tide
> When it's out it stinks
> When it's in it floods

Rich Red Velvet

Green and yellow and red and gold
With a taste of black to hue
I'm with your radiant beauty held
As I fondly gaze at you
So long your slim and shapely leg
In green of spring is draped
As I watch the yellow hot pant there
Covered o'er by your velvet cape
Such beauty rich of velvet red
Scarce has the Earths kings worn
So soft and splendid in all its glow
Changing softly from early morn
Your blouse of finest silken thread
Which your full self on is pressed
But a brighter sheen of velvet's red
And by satin softness caressed
A band of gold on your shoulder lies
Where your cape covers your face
Where the folds of rich red velvet tries
To steal you splendour and grace
Your lovely head is nestled deep
Among your plaited hair
So rich and black and thickly set
Compliments your face so fair
The movements of your grace-filled form
Your sheen just serves to increase

While from your tender lovely form
A fragrance exquisite's released
Oh nature you are such a marvel
As everywhere you show
In your painting of the smallest tree
To the flowers which you grow
You take the simplest of them still
And scatter them everywhere
To show beauty true to hardened hearts
Like in this spring tulip here.

At Last Oh GUS

At last oh GUS I'm freed
Oh Gus this is the last song
Of love I'll ever write
It's all about the reasons
Why you'll sleep alone tonight
It's all about the love I craved
Which you never shared
It's all about love's burning need
I'll take unto my grave
Yes Gus this is the last song
Of love I'll ever tell
About the heaven I sought to know
And the hell I knew so well
About the empty lonely times
When for you I'd ache and pine

And all about the you I loved
But seems could never find
Gus this is the last love song
Which will flow from my hand
For in it you may see at last
Love you could not understand
In words the pictures that I drew
May someday come to life
To show how proud I was of you
As friend, lover and wife
To maybe reach into the cold
Where your heart love hidden lies
Away from me forevermore
While alone I'm left despised
Oh Gus this is the last love song
Which warbles in my throat
In profound strains of loneliness
I belt out every note
In lost sad agony and pain
I die for what we knew
With just these words upon my lips
"Gus -- I always will love you"
So forgive me for this little song
Which fate now bades me sing
To tell in death of life's love tale
Of how you were my everything
My empty corpse at last may find
The rest which I never knew

And may the Gods bring you joy
Teach you to love one day true
Oh Gus this is the final words
Which my heart wants to outpour
The final gasping words of love
To the one whom I adore
You'll tell our children of our life
How it long could've been
Tell them that I love them all
Wish I could hold them close again
Teach them of the loveless years
I waited for your change
Teach them to give someone
The love you left estranged
Gus it's true you never knew
Love samples as a child
But oh I wish I wish so much
You would at least have tried
So goodbye Gus I leave you now
To go to my better life
Where hidden in the arms of death
I'll hold my final wife
Wrapped in the cold damp ground
Ne'er 'gain lonely to be
Cured from life's lovelessness
Alone, happy but free

'Tis Summer Time and Once Again...

'Tis Summer time and once again

Within my shell I crawl

I hide beneath this mask of mine

To protect my every all

For fragile lies the heart within

Which seeks for love's release

And when a love seeks for a love

Deep held secrets come unleashed

Down from the folds of life again

Can come the pasts that's been

To haunt and terrorize the mind

If confessed to one not friend

So deep within my chasm shell

Retreat I for safety's sake

Therein to live my living hell

Hiding so my heart won't break

For love I too did one time know

And hoped it long would last

Now only in name does it live on

Yet I'm tied to it so fast

Oh why can't life be kind but once
Release me and let me live
Pull back the blinds of time and let
Me be free once more to live

Remove the aching cancer which
My heart is dying from
Give me the chance to breathe again
And seek out a lasting love
If there but be a God above
Or one who guides our lives
Why can't they look upon this land
And remove the cause of cries
If death is near and hear my plea
Then stretch thy hand for me
For a lost lonely heart such as I
Would welcome you to set me free
Alas again in vain I call
Each day and night I live
Then crawl back in my empty shell
To await whate'er life will give...

Your Arms Reach Out to Hold Me...

Your arms reach out to hold me

Your sweet lips

Touch my own

I feel like a lost ship

Coming home

Your love it draws me to you

Your warmth

So full endures

I never feel

Like anymore to roam

But...

As the days grow longer

And our love grows

Deeper too

You will in time again

Say once to me

I'm yours forever darling

In every way you want

Tho I know

Husbands

Never set wives free...

Gossip Is No Artifact...

Gossip is no artifact
In fact it is no art
It's but a destruction of the facts
To pull somebody back down
It is no art to gossip speak
As facts they unneeded are
You simply take whatever you see
And stretch it near and far
You open both your ears and mouth
Each tidbit to embrace
No thought e'er given to the source
From which gossip vile escapes
Then quickly you begin to see
What you had hoped to find
You convict the innocent on lies
That were fed to your open mind
The greatest spot for gossip then
Is the hate-filled mind unseen
And the greatest cesspool to be filled
Is the receptive mind unkeen
For few too few will question straight
The basis if gossip they desire
But rather will in patience wait
To get all their minds require
But lastly there remains a few
Who are led by only fact
They forsake gossip for wisdom true
And they friendship never lack...

You Fly So Far and High Above...

You fly so far and high above
Without a sound you move
In your distant watchful waiting
O'er Sun and Stars and Moon
No one recalls your presence
Yet we know you once were here
By the bits of past life civilized
Which here and there appear
Your ways of moving over
Thru clouds and skies on high
Still causes awe and wonder
As swiftly you pass us by
Your means of propulsion
Doth our imagination shake
So fast you travel silently
No exhaust or sounds you make
Why can't we learn the secrets
Of ultra-motive force
To aid us in our quest to reach
Your elite and heavenly course
Perhaps it's best that we remain
Earthbound and that is why
So far you've kept your secrets
Safe hidden there on high
Yet one day U.F.O. captain
Your far realm I shall attain
And learn your deeper secrets
Tho then them I'll ne'er explain...

~~ April ~~

April...
Aye the month of true Spring
Trees budding
Robins chirping
Kids laughing
Life anew touching everything

Showers...
Falling waters from distant skies
Clean refreshing
New birth giving
Cold yesterday rejuvenating
Like tears of laughter in ladies eyes

Thunderclouds...
Dark foreboding with a threat
Lightning flashes
Thunderclap crashes
Treetop thrashes
'Round about all screaming wet

Serenity...
Nature's bowers of retreat
Calm collected

Soft protected
Warmth projected
From the moment we first meet

Electricity...
Flashes of life's fire flame
Warming welcomed
Destruction hindered
All by you contained
As but warmth flows from your flame

Like a motor
Needing opposite
Polarities each they interact
Like a magnet
Warm you draw me
Nearer tho I draw yet back

Feel your forces
Natural of nature
Cling to mine in unison
Each outreaching
The nearness wanting
Yet withdrawing each goes on

Free the forces
Let the Spring
All blossoms free
Fear not the lightning
Nor the crashing thunder
Fear not for in Spring it must be

See the new buds
Open willingly
Setting all their treasures free
See the new bee
Drink the honey
Leaves its sweetness pollen free

Yet too soon
The Summer cometh
May and June July pass by
Then it's back
To toil and worries
April's Spring has passed us by

April...
Aye the month of true Spring
Roses budding
Birds a-chirping
Children laughing
Reach out renew life for one thing...

Standing in the Dusklight...

Standing in the dusklight
Of another lovely day
I think
Of the peaceful serenity of it all
I wonder at its beauty
On hill and sky and by
And of other peaceful nights
I still recall
I can see again
The times I once knew
Times long gone past
With good friends warm and true
And their memories yet linger
In my mind

Thinking back to days
Now left behind
Like the wavelets
And the ripples on the seas
The best of friends must soon
Go on on their ways
Leaving naught
But happy memories
Still so often
I wish that they could stay

I recall with deep regret
And pain
All the good times
That never more can be
I must wander onwards
To my goal
Following ever
My first love
The sea

Yet at times I stand
And I think again
To another serene sunset
Gone... and then
In my heart
The pain of loneliness cries
As my memories past
Once more
In memories
Pass me by...

Cheating is not cheating when it results
from constant limits and refusals

Tho the Day Be Long and Dreary...

Tho the day be long and dreary
Tho the nights remain so cold
In my deepest thoughts your memory
Keeps me warm as it I hold
Tho you know not me nor I you
Yet your eyes they tell me true
Of your thoughts so deep and lovely
Flowing silently in you

Let remain as you have thought them
Let their gossip ne'er you change
Once in a while a flower blossoms
Without Sun or Earth or Rain
You a breeze-like cool approaches
Taking all life's cares away
Ah but so great our differences
We both know you can't stay

Yet for the time you do linger
Let my words say thank you dear
Friendship warm
Shines in your blue eyes
Every time I glance in there
Keep your way of life
And live it
And may happiness be your lot
Warmth and joy
And understanding
And the love that you have sought...

Golden Moon So Softly Shining

Golden Moon so softly shining
Upon the closed Canadian seas
You bring to me fond memories
Of other places I have seen
Your shimmering glistening waters
So softly murmur low
Telling me tales of bygone days
Spent in places I did go to
You touch upon the seashore
You touch upon the ship
You touch my heart forevermore
As I gaze at you each trip
You've put pure gold and silver
Upon the head of one I love
You bring my heart a quiver
Whene'er she's close to me like now
Yet in your cool cool glimmer
There lingers yet warmth true
As you touch my thoughts most inner
Teaching me to love anew
So shine on Moon on waters
Where e'er a lonely heart stands
Be they Canadian Icy waters
Or of the warm Caribbean lands
You'll do your duty truly
Of this I have no fear
And I'll be happy eternally
For Moon my friend you're near

I Watched and Yearned

I watched and yearned and waited long

To hold her loving body near

To feel the warm exuberance

That manifested itself clear

I thought of her and all I'd do

Of how things they could be

Of holding near her beauty warm

Of setting her fears free

At last she into my arms did fall

In sweet surrender soft

With purr like kittens mellow yawn

I heard her sweetly laugh

I touched her hands in love's caress

I held her close to me

The time I'd longed for and had hoped

Was given now to me

She was so warm and willing

My poor heart leapt with joy

Here new mine for the taking

Mine to love caress enjoy

Her sweet soft lips softly rested

Against mine as we stood

While a thousand thoughts raced thru my mind

Backed by the questions "should?"

Should I who had so long endured

The pain and sleepless nights

To have her willing to me come

To take her now had I the right

Should I the past of worshipness

Bring to an untimely end

Or would she remain e'er dear to me

As lover as when friend

I thought it over my mind was set

Too long I'd let her love run free

I kissed and said to save regrets

My love please marry me

Beyond That Far Horizon

The silver sea reflects the constant sun
While we take for granted all we see
We live our selfish useless lives
Without a thought of helping souls to free

But beyond that far horizon
One day we all must go
We'll meet there our Redeemer
And at last true joy we'll know
He will take our hand and lead us
Where the quiet waters flow
Just beyond that far horizon
Where we all must someday go

There are some who still chide Him
Some who feel that He's unreal
Others lay store in Earthly goods
'Cause they feel it's a better deal

So my friend or foe please listen
To the words of our Saviour dear
Turn your thoughts and works to Him
And we'll meet in Peace up there

So Strangely At Peace

As one watches the soft grey tranquility
of morning slowly give way to the red
gold of the morning's sun, the world
seems at peace so strangely at peace

As the low flying birds skims reflection
close to the gossamer waters causing
never a ripple there on their beauty is
doubly obvious and the world seems
at peace so strangely at peace

As the first soft ripples break the glass
-- like finish of the gold tinted waters
one is aware of the marine life which stirs
below in their aquatic splendour and still
the world seems so strangely at peace

Then the mornings suns glow fills all the
silent spaces filtering thru the wisps of
grey fluffy morning clouds bent it seems
only on awakening the world and nature once
more to remove the cloak of peacefulness
which covers it so strangely

Alas there sounds an unfamiliar loud and
heavy droning as man and his machines
invade in full the pregnant silence which
the world did in such peaceful splendour lay

Suddenly the peace, the tranquility and
the silent splendour is once more pushed
aside as the turmoil of everyday toil
sounds loudly and strangely the world no
longer now seems to be at peace

Brighter grows the day and louder yet the
invasion of these foreign sounds which lay
claim to the peacefulness of the predawn
and one wonders aloud why the world no
longer seems at peace

Yet as the sun sinks slowly downwards one
watches as the soft moon casts once more upon
the world its peace demanding glow then strangely,
slowly, but nevertheless so fully, the noises
of the daytimes seems to somehow dissipate
and blend into a new harmony to give way
once again to the calming call of night

The glow long gone now from the sun,

the foreign noises so subdued,

the soft moons light like polish new on a glassy

piece of art, once more the silent birds

flies low looking in the reflective waters

a mirror to them as the peacefulness reappears

And so another cycle in the wheel

of life has been completed another lovely

recall to those who pause to think

The world may with its turmoil and all its

works and pleasures remove but for a short

while the peacefilled sounds of silence,

remove for but a short while the peace

which in the world so softly sleeps

As one watches the soft grey tranquility

of morning slowly give way to the red gold

of the morning's sun, the world again is at

peace, tho only for a short time, the world

is so strangely, once again at peace

I Met a Face and Body Soft

I met a face and body soft

With warm and welcome arms

A heart that beat with love divine

Which would keep me ever from harm

A life of rosy paths ahead

A vision of bright days

These all are but things I recall

As at our memories I do gaze

I see the home that we had planned

I see the kids we crave

I even feel again it seems

Those soft caresses you gave

I thought that we would ever be

Free loving warm and true

I never thought the Winter's snow

Would fall on my heart from you

I never thought the many times

When you to my heart I pressed

That deep inside you were so filled

With doubt hate and deep regrets

I saw a boy so young and strong

Grow to a tall and stalwart man

To live and love enjoying life

'Twas his every hope and plan

But here you see in half score years

A body aged and broken bent

A cripple filled with loves decay

Paying hard for love just lent

The old and aged man you see

With head and shoulders down

Was once that tall and stalwart man

Who walked as man with all around

This broken hopeless unloved soul

Yes here forever I'll be

Less than a man, less than a man

You killed the man in me

Oh the Day It Is But Starting

Oh the day it is but starting
And the pains of home are strong
But I know it won't be long now
'Til I'll be a long time gone
I will walk by quiet waters,
Stand long by the old folk's graves
And recall the times I used to
Play among the palms that wave
Oh the day is bright its noontime
And the lapping waters fall
As I watch the songbirds telling
Of this home loved by us all
Oh the day at last is ending
As the evening sun goes down
As I head far deeper Southwards
My heart is glad I'm homeward bound
So my friends and others listen
But forget my days of woe
I've a home a land and country
Where better off I'll live I know
So you take your manmade pleasures
And you take your cold false ways
While I live amid earth's treasures
Warm and secure all of my days
Oh the day is but beginning
And the night's moonbeams dim grow
But my heart is full and worn now
'Cause I'm homeward bound I know

Talk About Matches and Menus

Talk about matches and menus

Allover the floor

Somebody done vex Joan

A-aint know what for

She's working so quiet

In she tiny booth

When she get sting by matchstick

Which somebody shoot

0 — 00 — 000 she arm swell up

An a fas'y fas'y officer

He so quick to speak up

Boy why come is no on she chest you hit

Ah would like fe see you swell them up a bit

At this she get furious

Ah she no like the remark

All the crew now was curious

To see she face all aspark

Den to the fas'y officer

She turn with a swear

Oh Lawd now there's matches

And menus most everywhere

Today for Just a Little While

Today for just a little while
I sat and gazed in awe
Becoming dumbstruck and perplexed
By the little things I saw
I live and know that all around
Were living growing things
From fishes trees insects and ants
To birds on soaring wings
But suddenly I chanced to glance
Up to the mountain side
And lo behold there I beheld
Still clouds -- the wind had died
Ne'er before can I recollect
Clouds of such small wisps to lie
Suspended and so motionless
Unmoving in the sky
The birds flew round to gaze it seems
Into the utter still
Of clouds like pictures in our dreams
A-clinging to the hill
No tree did move near anywhere
Waters ripples all were still
As I watched the clouds so motionless
The day the wind stood still
The paintings of the evening sky

Did paint faintly there on
Its new and changing evening scene
Once more -- then moved along
The ships and boats and birds all
Moved on water and thru the air
Yet still thru all I gazed and gazed
Those lifeless clouds hung there
I knew then that I'd been allowed
As darkness hid my view
To see such as few men have seen
Tho they've lived their whole lives thru
I'd been by chance a memory given
To share as life goes by
To tell to all mankind who's living
One day the winds did die

Take my hand hold it
Take my mouth kiss it
Take my life control it
Take my heart love it
But Take Today as yours
Live it

A Wonderful Wonderous Woman

Into thy arms I slowly creep my love
No longer does my pride restrict me now
Your warmth your love your deep caress
I know will ever give me happiness
To live is to laugh to sing and to cry
To lose you would be to surely die
You are to me eternally
A wonderful wonderous woman

My eyes can clearly see again
My heart with joy beats in refrain
To the millions of songs which I sing
To the feelings of joy since you came in
To my life my love my every scheme
The wants of my waking the girl of my dreams
To me — you'll remain — eternally
A wonderful wonderous woman

Tho others my life did once possess
Like heaven you gave me a perfect rest
You've beat all the others so easily
In loving and caring Grace for me
You destroyed all the doubt that I once knew
As a wife and lover and mother so true
That proud am I with you by my side
Forever — Forever — with me to abide
I loved you last — but eternally
You wonderful wonderous woman

Hi Love

Hi Love

When I see you so small

Enter in this world of mine

Near and warm and lovely

Dear and darling to us all

Your ways are all so constant

Moving in your graceful way

Thru work and play and wonder

To reach goals you've sought today

Reach on then for higher places

In your world or else in mine

Soon you'll leave my side forever

On your journeys thru life wide

Never look then back in wonder

At the dreams past cast aside

Only set to shape your future

Run along the paths you've set

Young in heart in mind in body

On You must your dreams protect

Until You my heart it can forget

You Look At Me and Your Eyes See

You look at me and your eyes see

But louder yet do they speak

Deep questions you would ask of me

Which in your mind doth creep

Then we hold for but a moment

In deepest thoughts ourselves

But too soon that thought is spent

As individually we return ourselves

Yet tell me what do you retain

From those soft deep moments shared

Be not afraid they'll ne'er be known

By anyone for whom you've cared

While I go on -- my way alone

Yet, for a moment of time it seemed

That fused our time did wait

Suspended in a pleasant wakeful dream

Which we have seen too late

Just for a while it seemed to me

The sun played warm upon my face

Bringing its beauty and joy to me

As I gaze at your lovely face

Ah but alas your eyes they move

And reality to me returned

But heaven was visible in the grove

While from your eyes I'd learned
I'd learned of thoughts I keep deep
Of words I would love to say
Of an eternal rendezvous I'd keep
With someone like you every day
But alas 'tis but a vision swept
Away, by your passing glance
But 'tis a memory of mine deeply kept
In hopes of some future chance

If Only

If only I could write my thoughts of you
Say what you want to hear from me
Be where you desire me
Do what you ask of me
Hold you as you need me
Live what you want me to be
Circumstantially change me
Then the complexities of our lives would not be
But since I cannot write nor say nor be
Nor do nor hold nor live
Nor circumstantially change
What my master fate has planned
Then I will love thee pure distant chaste and afar

Heart of Life's Long Yearning

Heart of life's long yearning
Dreams of what could be
Hopes of loves long yearnings
Dashed away once more from me
Thoughts of times that's ahappening
Smiles of days so few
Heart of life's long yearnings
Reawakened friend by you
Symbol of the Yuletide
Fairest kissed by mornings dew
Complimented by the Ivy
Which is o'ershadowed far by you
Soft and wavy, lithe and fragile
Like a petal from a rose
Brightening life's dark corners
Most everywhere you go
So like life's remembrance twiglets
Which from your name 'twas taken
You bring down Sun Stars and moonlets
To grace your sky-blue eyes of heaven
Is it any wonder then that Humans
Such as I in awe doth stand
For a chance to hold your beauty

For a hope to hold you in hand
I who long have searched thru gardens
In my quest for beauty rare
Stand aghast now that I've found it
Stand staring at your face so fair
Cast aside not my long held hope
Cause my dreams not to be vain
Life it shares with us but seldom
Joy and love for suffered pains
So Heart of life's long yearnings
As again to you I turn
Cast your eyes upon mine searching
For a dream whereto to turn
Heart of life's long yearnings
May your life be filled with love
Heavy o'er life's long years unchanging
Happy e'er as you look now

Always around in my memories
Pausing playfully in my thoughts
Recalling reverent moments shared
In inner circles secretly ours
Living lingering longing memories

Peggy, Mary, Marie and Me

Peggy, Mary, Marie and me

Three girls and their old used to be

Robert, Walter and Jimmy

Took my first three loves from me

I was happy I was free

Peggy, Mary, Marie and me

Now I've got nowhere to go

Nothing to do

You see

Please come back

I'm so lonely

For Peggy, Mary, Marie and me

I could have had Jeanne

I could have had Ruth

Joan calls Gracie waits

But I'll tell the truth

There's no one much I care to see

Half as much as

Peggy, Mary or Marie

Someone said the far stars could be reached

This is your day to reach and pick them

Happy Why Not

Happy why not it's your birthday
Another year of loves labour has passed
Another year of fond memories building
Another year to improve over the past
Another year to dream and to ponder
The mysteries of life and of love
Another year to gaze in starry-eyed wonder
At life's beauties around you like now
Happy why not it's your birthday
And I hope that it in may be
Filled with all the things you desire
And that one of those things will be me
Somewhere in your thoughts or actions
Somewhere in your laughter so free
Spare a small moment to Darling remember
How much you're loved truly by me
Happy I hope so, it's your birthday
And your presence in my arms will tell
That I wish you just 'nough more to keep you
'Til I on this Earth cease to dwell
For be it short or long life is loving
And without you that would seem wrong
So have a Happy, Happy Birthday Darling
And may each new one repeat this love song

Well Here I Am Again

Well here I am again
Right where it all began
The sand the sea the boats
The cars the logs the trees
The kids the sounds
The buildings -- ah -- alas
Yes the buildings
The buildings overlook the beach
With four windows all a-front
Thru which they reach for food
The sunseekers one and all
They reach for food
The parking lot not yet quite filled
The air still by winter chilled
And yet they wander along
In search of sunshine
Sand castles and goose pimples all
Intermingle as you see them small
They lie basking in the early heat
Trying some elusive goal to reach
Some bronze tanned body to secure
Which will last 'til Summer's over
Knowing it cannot natural
This tanning
Two here two there

With kids that abound
The women lie and sun
One wonders if this daily task
Will be worth the evening's burn
With faces up and faces down
Like roasts on spits they turn
To catch a bit of healthy brown
From the e'er elusive sun
Lifeguards rake the beach of moss
To while the hours away
While pigeons, seagulls, coal black crows
O'er the fresh raked seashore play
One questions why the same goes on
Ne'er change from year to year
The place the people's faces all
It seems the same appears
But then mayhap like homing birds
They return here yet to roost
The never changing Spanish Banks
This place Sunseekers choose

A poem is the poets private place for putting
past personal pictures of life in proper perspective

Come Here

Looking at her softly he quietly said
"Come here"... and then...

Just for a moment
One short split-second in time
She started to rise and obey
Then as her two soft hands
Held open her heart's door
She slumped back back and away.

In a prison of memories
Deep down in her mind
Built on conventions she knew
She hides from her feelings
She hides from herself
She hides there from love ever true.

Stuck by the voices of childhood
Restricted by parsonage ways
Living in the shadows of others
E'er conscious of what they may say
Afraid to live love and be happy
Afraid to crawl out of her shell
Afraid of her womanly feelings
Afraid they'd condemn her to hell.

Step out to my world he tells her
Step out and let me lead you anew
There's a big open world yours awaiting
If your prison doors you but step thru
Reach out, you alone them can open
Reach out, help yourself and we'll share
Life waits for none but the living
Love calls not too often "Come Here".

I Received the Answer

I received the answer to my letter
I'm sorry that we had to part this way
But if you feel he can love you better
I'll be content to live alone always
It's just that it hurt so deeply
To hear you say the words I used to hear
And to think you're saying them unregretfully
For a friend that I once thought dear
If someday you should remember
The kind of love tho short that we once shared
You could come back home
I'll still be there alone
Living my life alone always

Come Sit Awhile

Come sit awhile on yonder rock
As sunlight golden streaks your hair
And I shall bare my soul to thee
In words of natures whispers clear
Come sit and of the birds I'll tell
As each one sings thy name in song
And warbles to its mate in understanding
The truth which you have brought along
Come sit and watch the tall trees growing
Each living it seems with one accord
To reach e'er up their crowning glory
In reverence and worship unto God
Come sit and listen to the brooks sing
As o'er each rock and stone they flow
Telling tales of places they have been to
And beauties rare of which they only know
Come sit awhile with me and nature
As we invade and then a part become
Come join us in the unending clatter
Of time as it so silently goes on
Come sit awhile here beside me
Let me in silence gaze you upon
That deep within my heart will be singing
In praise your beauty in a song

Come sit awhile where deer wander

In play as Spring falls upon the air

As does give life anew to fawnlings

And blossoms fragrance fills the air

Come sit awhile here in this bower

And I shall reach for you in love

To too become a part here of nature

As we become as nature two in love

Then as Spring's sun touches the hilltops

Long the shadows of the trees appear

They'll seem to be but knees abending

As upright still held are their heads in prayer

Come sit awhile here besides me

All of nature's wonders with me share

Let us enjoy the tranquil peace of nature

As side by side we tarry silent here

Come sit while here love beside me

And in words silent I shall sing thee song

And God and nature shall bear witness

That like the peaceful silence love lives on

Boys are born boys and grew into men
Women are just born

Other Collections by This Author:

A Poet's Ebb And Flow

... and Touches Of Nature

In The Middle of Believe There's A Lie

Inside A Heart

Judge Me Not Without A Trial

Legends, Lives & Loves Along the Inside Passage

Love... Life's Illusive Zenith

Love's Refuge and Sonnets

Only Children Of The Universe Are We

Step Scenes Of Life

That We Too Free May Live

~ ~

For more information go to:

w w w . d n c s i t e . c a

~ ~

www.ingramcontent.com/pod-product-compliance
Lightning Source LLC
Chambersburg PA
CBHW021343090426
42742CB00008B/725